SUNSHINE BLACKROSE

Aliscia Melton

SUNSHINE BLACKROSE

From Origination to Maturation
A Transformation in Poetic Form

ALISCIA MELTON

SOUTH CAROLINA

Aliscia Melton

Copyright © 2015 by Aliscia Melton.

Published by Sunshine BlackRose Publications
928 Shearwater Way, Warrenville, SC 29851
www.SunshineBRPublication.com

All rights reserved. Printed in the United States of America. No part of this book may be used or reproduced, stored in a retrieval system or transmitted in any manner whatsoever without written permission. The only exception is brief quotations in printed reviews.

Cover design by BRPP Custom Designs

ISBN: 978-0692512050

0692512055

POETRY IS…..

The beginning of my day and the end of my night

It is that calm in the midst of a storm

It is the sparkle at the beginning of a rainbow just after the rain

It is the sigh inked out after a hardship is felt

It is that pressure valve when one wants to explode

It is the joy of bringing happiness and hope to your fellow man

Poetry is my mind spillage

Words overflowing

My Heart and Life

DEDICATION

I dedicate this book to Life, Mercy, Grace, and Favor

Life for teaching me so many lessons

Mercy for sparing me in my wayward, backsliding, confused, and lost days

Grace for covering me with the free and unmerited favor of God.

Favor for it isn't always fair but I humbly and graciously accept it and walk boldly in its beautifully colored garment that I have been blessed with.

CONTENTS

INTRODUCTION ix

Prologue………………………………………………...…..xi

CHAPTER ONE 15

CHAPTER TWO 31

CHAPTER THREE 47

CHAPTER FOUR 61

Epilogue 75

Acknowledgments 79

About the Author 81

INTRODUCTION

This book is a brief glimpse into my life and the transformation God has made thus far.
It is a journey from the origination of Sunshine BlackRose to realization of life. That realization leads to maturation which brings about the transformation of Sunshine BlackRose.

Come and peek in, read, and ride along with Sunshine BlackRose as she blossoms into a strong force to be reckoned with. He's not done yet so to be continued and watch out world because here I come!

Aliscia Melton

Prologue

PLANTED SEED PT 1

UMM HE HAS GREAT PLANS FOR HER
I MUST GET TO WORK EARLY I SEE
ROB HER OF HER FATHER
MOLEST HER OF HER INNOCENCE
CREATE ROADBLOCKS FROM HER NURTURER
TAKE AWAY HER SELF WORTH
THIS ONE COULD BE POWERFUL IF I DON'T KILL HER IN HER YOUTH!
PLANT SEEDS OF INFERIORITY
AND ONES OF MISTRUST
DROP THAT SEED OF ABANDONMENT
YEAH THIS WILL KEEP HER IN THE DARK
HAHAHA
YES COME TO ME MY PRECIOUS
STAY WITH ME HERE IN THE SHADOWS
AS I WHISPER IN YOUR EAR WITH THESE PERNICIOUS THOUGHTS
YOU KNOW YOU AIN'T WORTHY
YOU KNOW YOU AIN'T SHIT
GIRL, THEY DON'T LOVE YOU
THEY JUST USE YOU WHEN IT FITS
GIRL WHY YOU WAITING
JUST END YA MISERY NOW!!
POP THOSE PILLS DRINK THAT DRINK
WHY CONTINUE THIS LIFE OF WRETCHEDNESS
YOU NEED TO END IT NOW!
WHAT DOES IT REALLY MATTER
NO ONE WILL MISS YOU ANY HOW.....
YOU ARE ALL ALONE
SO JUST END IT NOW!

SUNSHINE BLACKROSE

*From Origination to Maturation
A Transformation in Poetic Form*

Aliscia Melton

CHAPTER ONE

ORIGINATION

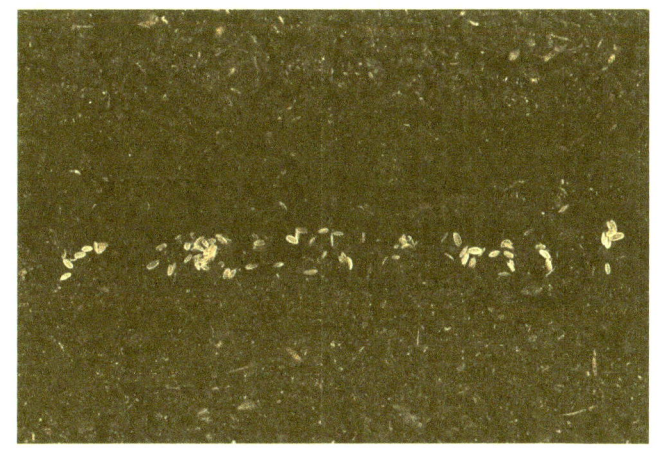

HE AND SHE LOVED
REPRODUCTION
FERTILIZATION
POLLINATION
BLACK ROSE'S ORIGINATION IS..

BLACK ROSE

A SEED WAS DROPPED AMONGST THE DIRT AND ROCK IN
THE CRACKS AND CREVICES OF THE COLD CONCRETE OF
LIFE
THERE MY ROOTS WERE ESTABLISHED, IN A DRY PLACE
NOT HAVING THE PROPER WATER AND SUNLIGHT TO
FLOURISH
BUT STILL I GREW
UNDER THE CLOUDS OF DARKNESS FEEDING
TAKING NOURISHMENT FROM THE MOONLIGHT
ROOTS STRONG AND FIRM
I AM A BLACK ROSE
WITHSTANDING THE RAIN AND STORMS
THE TRAMPLING OF FEET
THE DIRT AND TRASH
FOR I AM NOT SEEN
I AM NOT BRIGHT, COLORFUL
RED, YELLOW, OR WHITE
BUT A ROSE IS STILL A ROSE
I AM A BLACK ROSE
WHAT CAN WITHSTAND THE DARKNESS
TAKE ROOT IN SQUALLER
BREAK THRU THE COLD CONCRETE
TO BUD, BLOSSOM, AND FLOURISH
FINDING ITS WAY TO SUNLIGHT
NOTHING BUT A BLACK ROSE
FOR A ROSE IS STILL A ROSE
BEAUTIFUL AND PRECIOUS
PETALS SOFT AND SMOOTH AS PURE SILK
DELICATE WITH A SWEET AROMA
I AM A BLACK ROSE
SEE THE LIGHT SHINE ON ME
FOR I HAVE FOUGHT HARD TO REACH HIM
WE HAVE FINALLY FOUND EACH OTHER
NOW ALL CAN SEE THE TRUE BEAUTY IN ME
FOR I WILL ALWAYS BE
A BLACK ROSE

DADDY'S GIRL

Daddy's girl
Daddy's girl
Who doesn't want to be a daddy's girl
Running to the door because daddy's home
Receiving all the extra hugs and kisses
Piggy back rides around the house while mom is cooking
in the kitchen
The bed time stories and being kissed and tucked in at
night
Him telling you "don't let the bed bugs bite"
Climbing in his lap feeling safe and secure
Daddy daughter dances, for sure, you always went
Him wiping your tears from that first breakup
You making his coffee in his favorite cup
The pride he feels sending you off to college
You racking up mileage
On that new car he gave you
Tears of joy as he walks you down the aisle
Him telling you you're beautiful making you smile
Your special dance at the wedding where he holds you
tight and you both cry
Reminding each other this is not a good bye
Just a new chapter in life
The excitement and love you seen in his eyes

When you tell him the big surprise
His new name will be Grandpop
When he holds your child for the first time and the tears won't stop
Reading to him as he once did for you
Now you're taking care of him, who knew
Daddy's girl
Daddy's girl
Who doesn't want to be a daddy's girl
What I wouldn't do to be a daddy's girl
All I have is a song
(Singing) M-E-L-T-O-N spells Melton
Him teaching me to proudly spell our name
That memory I will hold on to forever
And our name, I plan on taking to the Hall of Fame

Mommy

She is a woman of beauty
A woman of strength
Her love reaches great lengths
And goes to the deepest of depths
Her sacrifices, too many to count
Overflowing….
Her Love is a fount
Mommy
Today is a day to appreciate you
Because your love is tried and true
You never gave up on us
And said you were through
You will always be my #1 boo!
Who knew
After all that we have been through
I thank God for you
For our relationship He did mend
You have become my best friend

Sisters Bond

Ride or die for my sisters
Shed blood for my sisters
Go to the ends of the earth for my sisters
Catch a case for my sisters
Protect and cover my sisters
My first assignment in life
My sisters
Attempting to come between us is absurd
Our bond can't be broken
Thicker than thieves
Tougher than leather
We ride or die in all kinds of weather
We are altogether
Lovely
Giving you a run for ya money like Mayweather
But we definitely ain't no light feathers
Feather weights, wait
We are in a class of our own
Pound for Pound
Blow for blow
We be on that physicadelacal flow
Supernatural connect setting us aglow
That's why I ride or die for my sisters
Shed blood for my sisters
Go to the ends of the earth for my sisters
Nothing but straight love for my sisters

Memories of Mommom & Poppop's house

Beautiful fall days playing outside in the leaves
The laughter as we jump into the piles we created
Good times like these is so underrated
Closing my eyes I can see the red, orange, and browns of the season
Smell the crisp air of the fall season
Reminiscing makes my love for this place deepen

Hot summer days spent in the pool
Trying to stay cool
Laying in the grass allowing the sun's rays to dance off the lids of our closed eyes
As our chlorine drenched and shriveled bodies dried

The warm comforting smell of the wood burning stove in the winter
The time spent with mommom removing the splinters
Received from helping poppop bring in the wood
Oh if only I could…
Go back to those days
Bring them back like replays

Fixing poppop's coffee
Mixing in the sugar and cream until it's the color of toffee
The feeling of accomplishment when you get his approval
"Just the way I like it" he says with a big kiss on the forehead

Helping mommom cut up potatoes for dinner
I just knew I was a winner
Sneaking bits of food when she wasn't looking
How I miss her good ol' home cooking
Watching mommom plant her spring flowers
And poppop weed the garden

While me and my cousins ran around the backyard like we had super powers
These joyous memories will never be forgotten

There was no better place on earth to be but here
At Mommom and Poppop's house......
The place I will always call home

Wedding Day

June 17, 1995
My wedding day
The day I walk down the aisle
To say
I do with a big smile
Close friends and family are all gathered
To watch Bishop Lassiter unite us in holy matrimony
Us both thinking, now we will never be lonely
June 17, 1995
We made a wow to death do us part
And to forever protect each other's heart
Just knew we were destined from the start
June 17, 1995
My wedding day
Marrying the man of my dreams
Ride or die, by all means
The day filled with food, fun, and laughter
Just knew we would live happily ever after
June 17, 1995
My wedding day

Naked

I stand before you defenseless
-No Armor
-No Sword
-No Shield
-No Walls
In my rawest form
Unprotected and vulnerable beyond measure
Surrendering, Presenting, and Placing
In your hands
All of my precious jewels
-My Heart
-My Mind
-My Soul
-My Spirit
-My Emotions
-My Insecurities
-My frailties
-My Body
Please handle with care

Why

I give all of me to you.

Shower you with love, affection, and attention.

You are my only desire, my first priority.

Wash your clothes

cook your dinner, bring you your plate

Massage your stress away

Even fulfill all your lustful desires

I pour all of my being and heart into you

So please tell me.....

Why am I not enough for you???

???

DO YOU WANT ME OR NOT???
MAKE UP YOUR MIND
STOP PLAYING THESE LOVE GAMES
CONFUSED AND IN PAIN
IS HOW YOU CHOOSE TO LEAVE ME EACH DAY
DO YOU WANT ME OR DON'T YOU??
STOP PLAYING THESE LOVE GAMES
ONE MINUTE YOU ADORE ME
LOOK AT ME WITH EYES OF ENDEARMENT
THEN YOU CAN'T STAND ME
CUSS ME OUT AND ABANDONED ME....
MY HEART IS IN SHAMBLES
BEWILDERED BY YOUR ACTIONS
IS IT PRIDE TALKING??
OR TRULY YOUR INTENTIONS??
TO HURT ME AND CONFUSE ME
TO PLAY WITH MY EMOTIONS
DO YOU WANT ME OR NOT??
PLEASE
STOP PLAYING THESE LOVE GAMES!!!

Little Girl

Vulnerable

Scared

Hurt

Little girl curled up in the corner

Trembling...

Shivering with fright

please don't hurt me...

Wanting only to be loved

Someone please come rescue me from within the shadows

of darkness

Defeat

Fear

Rejection

Hovering overhead

Spirit of depression whispering in her ear

Damn why is this little girl still living inside of me!

Pondering Thoughts

Pondering thoughts of why consume her day

Why did I not feel loved?

Why didn't my mother hold me?

Why did my father abandoned me?

Why did my husband not cover me?

Why did he strip me of my dignity and leave me?

Why, Why, Why?

Why me Lord??

Mistreated

Abandoned

Abused

Molested

Deceived

Forgotten

Why?

BECAUSE IT IS NOT ABOUT YOU MY CHILD, BUT ABOUT HOW I CAN USE YOU FOR MY GLORY. FOR YOU TO BE A LIGHT AND AN EXAMPLE OF HEALING AND DELIVERANCE, A SURVIOR IN THE WORLD.

Wishful Thinking

Wishful thinking of living in a whimsical winter wonderland
Has got me in a whirl wind of violently wild tornadoes
Now I'm writing tongue twisters about the tremendous turbulence
of my souls torturous adventures
Violently venting, spitting and spinning these words like spider
venom
A delusional warped whizzled web of deception I did weave in
my need
To successfully succeed at seemingly having a perfect life
A life lived lost at all cost caught up in fantasies of fairy tales
Resembling an ass' tail who sees through rose colored glasses
Telling tales that lead down wrong trails
My ass always attempting at aligning the atmospheric
constellations of reality
Praying secretly, silently at stretching the alignment of the stars
So I can be the gold star shining
Constantly ciphering through seasonal catastrophes
I am the wearer of this wondrous weather and cannot tell
whether I'm coming or going
Tossed to and fro in the tornadoes tunnels
Where I end up , no one knows

CHAPTER TWO

REALIZATION

LET GO, HOLD ON?
REBUILDING ALONE IS SO DIFFICULT......
REALIZATION

Speak to me Lord

Speak to me oh Lord,
Speak to me
I am in the dark
I need to hear a Word from you
So I dig deep into my heart
Searching for your words that have been planted there from the start
Oh how I need to be comforted
Lord please help me to regurgitate your Word!!
What is it that You've poured into me though out the years of my life??
When I sat at your table and you fed me the Bread of Life.
Oh how I need those words as I struggle to find my way out of darkness ….back into the glorious light
Was it that You'll never leave me nor forsake me??
That in my times of trouble you would be a refuge and my strength??
That you are my hiding place and will encompass me with songs of praise??
That I could find rest in you??
That you are my light and salvation??
Yes!!
I hear you Lord!!
It is all coming back!
Your Word has never left me
You have always been here
You ARE my strong tower
And I am running to You for safety.
You ARE my Light and Salvation
And I'm coming out of the dark!!

My cross

Face: Happy
Disposition: Cheery
"This too shall pass"
"You know I will always have your back"
Dying inside
But no one will know
I must be strong for everyone else
For that is my cross to bear:
Uplift the downtrodden….
Send inspiration into the world….
Pour into others……
Be that shoulder to cry on……
But whose shoulder can I cry on?
Who will pour back into me?
When I am empty, who will see about me?
That position has yet to be filled
So suck it up Liscia!
Fix ya face and get back out into the world!
You have a job to….
People need you.
(Shoulders back, smile on face)
"Hey babe!"
"How are you?"
"Yeah, I understand your pain."
"You know it will be OK."
"I am praying for you."
"Lay your head on my shoulder,
Let me relieve you of your pain and burdens."

Broken Pieces

I have been shattered
Slammed into the hard, cold pavement of Life and
Love
Broken into a million tiny pieces
Unable to love or accept love again
So it seems.......
Can I be mended? Put back together??
Will there always be missing shards of my heart?
Will I be just a portion of who I once was?
Who I could be?
How do I put my heart back together?
Can it truly be mended by a soul mate's gift of their
very own heart?

Am I Losing my Mind

Am I losing my mind?
Am I asking too much?
Are my expectations so high that no one will ever come close?
Will this lead to me being alone for the rest of my life?
Is it too much to ask for?
Loyalty
Commitment
Acknowledgement
Stability
Understanding
Support
And
Unconditional Love
Am I high maintenance- Requiring too much affection and attention? Am I damaged goods- Not able to let go of the past?
Or am I just a woman that knows her worth?
Refusing to settle for nothing less than what she deserves?
These are the questions that consume my mind
When contemplating God's great design
For My Love Life
So I bow my head
Get on my knees
Bask in His presence
Seeking his face
Asking for clarity and peace
As I patiently wait for His answer
To all my pleas

He is...

He is all that I need...

The Alpha and Omega

My beginning and my end

The cure to everything

He is the one that soothes my soul when it is aching

The balm in Gilead

Refreshing and breathe taking

My quiet peace during the storm

My solid rock and foundation

The giver of life

My Savior

There is no one like Him

Jesus..... You are so worthy of all my praise!

Love is.....

Love is.....

Honoring
Accepting
Caring
Protecting
Treasuring
Forgiving
Respecting
Nurturing
Giving
Receiving
Cherishing
It is....
Kindness
Humble
Unconditional
Uncensored
And
Everlasting
It covers a multitude of wrongs
Love is......Love
It is an action word
Something to be carried out not just stated.
So learn to walk the walk and not just talk about the walk
Of this precious journey called....
LOVE

Side Chick Foolishness

Ain't it funny how the side chick thinks she can replace the wife?
Even when wife chooses to remove herself, she still in that place
Chick you need to recognize
Just exactly what , yes I said what you were and are
A distraction, a moist hole, with itchy ears willing to believe all the lies being told to you
Thinking, "Awww, he is such a good man. I can give him all that he is missing."
Not understanding, you ain't even capable of fulfilling half of what he is getting
Being played…deceived …such a gullible ass
You have been used and abused but somehow you continue to return
Always with the thought that you can be more, hell better than the one HE has CHOSEN to marry
LOL
Ain't it funny how you calling the wife trying to tell her all about HER husband
Girl you've known him for 6 months.. texting and talking on social media
She's built a life, raised children, seen the good, bad, and ugly of that man
Been there when he had nothing, becoming a Mann. To inspire and uplift that Mann.
You don't know the half of that man
And you thinking you got the upper hand
HAHAHAHA
Girl, please, he will never be "your" man
Wifey got smart and moved on from the games
And here you are holding on…. SMH so lame
Now you figuring you won "your" man to only be told
"You and me… nah that ain't my plan" by that man!
You could never be a wife
You settle too much, sweetie, you ain't built for that life
No backbone or strength to stand up for yourself
So how could you possibly support, uplift or even build up a man???

Swearing that your shit don't stink and what's between your legs is better than the next
Never understanding that it takes more to keep a man
Actually have a man
Than what trick you can perform in the shadows of the night
Giving him thrills and chills
Tell me.....what are you getting?? Some paid bills??
Intellect, Strength, and Virtue is what it takes to hold him down
So while you concentrating on twerking
He's building a life with a woman who's working
And has her own, adding to the kingdom
Not lying on her back, wanting to receive from the kingdom
You should have listened to the wife, when you stepped to her with your foolishness
Opening your mouth oh too soon
Beating on your chest like you were the new lioness here to rule and graze and take over her pride land
Now look at you.....
Heart broken
In love with another's husband
Left all alone out in the wilderness with no real covering
The real Lioness has left the pride with the spot to be filled
And yet The King has not put you in that place still...
So if you are willing you lick your wounds, and understand you are just a cub
This Lioness might just be willing to take you in...
Prepare you and teach you to someday be all that she is...
Queen, Ruler, Lioness over your own pride land

So there just may be hope for you to be upgraded from Side chick to the only chick

Called... Wife

Roses are Red

Roses are Red

And this intimacy is Dead.....

Roses are Red

So is the teary blood shed

Wondering if this romance is truly dead

Could this image of rose covered beds

And soft sensual encounters all be a thing of the past

How something so blissful can vanish oh so very very fast

What for most is a picture of romance

Is for me a reminder of NOmance

Roses are Red

And this intimacy is Dead.....

Aliscia Ann Melton

Bullets filled with words and deeds meant for destruction flying
Lost in the cross fire
She gave up herself
Changing her name trying to find self in someone else
Never realizing He had already established who she would be
And given her all she ever needed right there during her birth
Presenting it to her in that name on that government certificate:
Aliscia Ann Melton

To My Unborn Children

I am sorry I didn't love myself enough to wait for your seed to be planted inside of me at the right time by the right man

So there I sat at 13 then 14, then 15 ona bus, in a cab on a secret trip to another state with a man 7 years older than me to have you sucked/vacuumed from my womb. Not once but 3 times. How I remember the dates of when you all should have been born, wondering what your faces looked like.

I am sorry I didn't love myself enough to protect you from your father's anger at you growing in my belly because he didn't want any more children. Him attacking me leaving you no more than bloody clumps as I bleed out on the bathroom floor all alone.

I am sorry that God blessed me with twins, and I was so scared of bringing you two into the world to meet your 2 brothers and 1 sister with a man that I knew wanted no more children. I was terrified bringing you into a decaying marriage, and I wasn't sure I could do it all alone. I complained about petty stuff like car seats and having to buy a new car that I fear God punished me by taking you both, my blessings, from me.

I am sorry for not loving myself enough to stand up, and not let a man force me to have a surgery that would not allow me to ever have children again. So that when that one that loved me and mine came along I could bring you into the world with a loving home and father.

To all my unborn children, I am sorry I was not strong enough to speak up for you, to protect you…

Even from myself I pray you all forgive me.

Spring Cleaning

Lord, help me to clean out all of the hurt from my heart. Give me the strength to power wash, and remove, all the negative words said to me from the crevices of my mind. Lord, give me the desire to let go of those who have let go of me. Help me to remove the sense of responsibility for them. Heal me from these lingering viruses of needing answers and closure that I may never receive. Clear out all of the clutter and distractions that are keeping me from doing your will. Lord, create a new and clean heart in me; renew my mind placing only things of you in it. Replace the clutter in the closet of my mind and heart with things that are honest, pure, just, lovely, virtuous, and of good report.
Things that are praise worthy.
Lord, my spirit is in need of spring cleaning.
Empty me of the old and fill me with a fresh anointing.
Take me down in the water again, baptizing me anew.
Amen.

Rose Colored Glasses

I see through rose colored glasses
More like rose colored ashes
My eyes have been trained
To see no strife or pain
Childlike eyes
Keeps the heart from coming to a demise
But roses do wither
Allowing you to see a sliver
Of reality…that makes you quiver
Leaving a nasty taste
So bitter
I see through rose colored glasses
More like rose colored ashes
My perception of life crashes
I've fallen….Look at all my scratches
Been bruised for ages
Had me thinking outrageous
Now I'm raging
Really not trying to be courageous
Heart bleeding out
Giving me much to write about
Ink well full
Trigger pulled
Crimson stained poetic bullets
Filling up booklets
Of my mind spillage
These words are the illest
Creating chaos and pillage
All in the village
I'm killin it
No more rose colored glasses
I'm the villain
Lividly Spillin

Sick
Where's the penicillin
Taking no prisoners
In my painful rummage
This is a violent scrimmage
My rose colored glasses
Has diminished
Totally blemished
No more happy image
Taking away all the fake gimmicks
Nothing is off limits
She is no longer timid
Leaving a strong lineage
Once accomplished
Then I'll lay it down
No more bullets
I'm finished

CHAPTER THREE

MATURATION

PAIN, GROWTH, STRUGGLE
LEADS TO MATURATION
OF SUNSHINE BLACKROSE
VICTORIOUSLY BLOSSOMING

Enough

He will not put on you more than you can bear is how the saying goes…
So when is enough enough?
And in asking that question am I wrong?
Am I not having faith in God??
Year after year, for the last 6-7 years (I have lost count now it has been way too much to grasp) someone has passed and things have been stripped from me….
Family members
Possessions
Identity
Friends
"Church family"
Sanity
Even attempted to steal my self-worth and kids
Death after death, relationship after relationship
Destruction and deception
When is enough enough????
Who has the say on exactly how much one can bear??
I can bear??
What is it that you are trying to show me Lord?
Why all the pressure, why all the pain?
Why strip me of all you have allowed me to accomplish and achieve?
Why leave me out here in the wilderness alone starting from scratch at the age of 38??
Why Lord??
Why??
I know you have a plan for my life.
I know you have called me to do Your work.
Please show me how that is possible in the state that I am in now.
MY CHILD, YOU ARE EXACTLY WHERE I WANT YOU TO BE….
MY GRACE IS SUFFICIENT FOR THEE: FOR MY STRENGTH IS MADE PERFECT IN WEAKNESS
BE STILL AND KNOW THAT I AM GOD……

Pure Gold

It's like the world tried to hold me back

Kill me as a child

But still I rose

With every blow of hate, pain, abuse, and dishonor

I took it all

Blow by blow

It almost had me beat

I was almost swallowed by defeat

But instead each blow made me stand taller

Stronger

Able to withstand the heat

Tossed in the fire

Not realizing it would only make me stronger

Burning me

Leaving only the pure and strong

So now what you see before you is nothing but pure unadulterated

gold!!

Peace in the storm

Chaos all around
Every door closed in my face
Boxed in on every side
With no escape in sight
Waters are rising
And turning quite violent
There is no place for me to go
What am I to do…
Flail my arms, scream and holler
This changes nothing
The waters still rising
Waves still violent
Still trapped in this box of raging currents
The only thing to do is
Bow my head
And ask for peace while in the storm

Started from the Gutta now I'm here

Started from the gutta now I'm here
Flowing these fresh lines making you grin from ear to ear
Giving ya mind wet dreams wit my ink
Got ya going in circles trying to think
Started from the gutta now I'm here
Taking you to the school of Sunshine BlackRose
Better than any 4 year college, this fact no one can oppose
Demanding me to climb higher, excel to your level
My word verbiage is so deadly, burial time… you need to get that shovel
See I started from the gutta now I'm here
Worked hard to step up my game
Now this Queen, Sunshine BlackRose is ready for fame
Delivering illuminating light with just my thoughts and a pen
Here to save you all my friend
I started from the gutta now I'm here
Walking in my call to set this world ablaze with my internal Fire
So the rest of you all just need to retire

The Answer

Are you looking for that unconditional Love?
For someone to never leave you?
To always comfort you in your time of need?
Listen to you talk about everything and anything?
Hold you?
Never dangle your failures over your head?
Forgives you when needed?
That someone to confide in?
Be vulnerable with?
Bare your soul to?
Or maybe you are looking for that one to uplift you?
Bring you joy and a smile when you most need it?
Protect you, keep you safe, and provide for you?
To just love and accept you just as you are?
Help you overcome your hurt and pain?
That special someone to laugh, love, and cry with?
Well He has been waiting for you with His hand out stretched.
You see, He loves you so much that before you even knew you needed Him and began your search for Him, He died for you.
What many of us are searching, seeking, and longing for cannot be found in man.
Jesus is the only one that can truly fulfill that void in your heart.
Anything else would just be a substitute and the rivers of joy, happiness, peace you may feel will eventually dry out.
For He is Love. Without having the Love of Christ, you can never truly love another. Not even yourself.
So if you are searching for all of the above things and you want them in abundance……

Drink of the Living water and be loved, cherished, and fulfilled for all of eternity!

THE TRUTH

I crave for the TRUTH

Seek out the TRUTH

Like a drug addict I fiend for the TRUTH

Been covered in lies and deception since the day of my birth

So now I'm throwing blows and elbows breaking free from its clutches

Breathing in that fresh air…called the TRUTH

Wrapping my arms around it, like my life depended on it

I can't understand why one would run from the TRUTH

I'm running full steam toward the TRUTH

Thanking God for the TRUTH

REBIRTH

Pain

Growth

Watch

Sunshine BlackRose

Blossom

Straight

To

Victory......

REBIRTH

Clothed in Grace

Look at her as she dances through life….
So whimsical
Movements of shear elegance
Agility
Poise
&
Finesse
Some may not understand how she can be so free
Maneuvering through the chaotic traffic of this world
Such suppleness
Light-footedness
Almost effortlessly….So it seems
For she is clothed in Grace
The free and unmerited favor of God
This beautifully exquisite and dazzling garment
A gift
Covering all of her infirmities
Making her Admirable
Radiant
&
Alluring
As she brilliantly blossoms wearing this cloak
Covered in the anointing of God
You see
Favor Ain't Fair
But it is humbly accepted and appreciated by her

I Wanna Hate You

I want to hate you so bad
You had the ability to fix our family
To make all wrongs right to heal all wounds to console our children
All with just a few words and a gentle touch
But no.. Pride
That evil demonic spirit got in the way
You still had/have the ability to soothe our baby girls pains
Wiping away her silent, invisible tears that stream down her face
To fill that void left in our son's heart repairing the damaged bridge between the 2 of you
You still have time to create a true and impenetrable bond with our baby boy.
The fate of a family you wanted, longed for, created, and asked God for
You walked away from and left all in shambles
You
The Man, Leader, Head of the Household
had the power to facilitate and lead us to healing.
To guide us to His presence, bringing us to the throne of grace, healing, repentance, and deliverance
But instead you chose to give up, abandon, walk away leaving us in a muddled mess
Me you could leave (wedding vows mean nothing today) but to leave your children in such states of confusion?
I wanna hate you so bad!!

But ….

Never hearing my pleas or cries
Me begging you to make it right with our babies
To stop being so self-absorbed in your own pain, anger, and mission to hurt me
That you have lost focus on your true mission in life...... Your children
Acknowledge your part in the pain we have caused in their lives
Drop the spirit of pride and put our children first
Not just in words
But in action
I wanna hate you sooo bad!
For leaving our family a train wreck

But....

I can't
God won't allow me to

My heart won't allow me to
So I will love you from a distance and continue to pray (and nag) you will create a relationship with our children that is beyond unbreakable.
A relationship like neither of us had with our fathers
You remember the kind we both so desperately craved for
That we wanted and needed
I wanna hate you so bad....

But...

I can't
God won't allow me to
Therefore, I have hope

The Real Strong Black Woman's Cry

Yes, I am a Strong Black Woman
I sure can hold my own
Strong
Powerful
Independent
Opinionated and Financially Stable
I can even be a Dominant Head of House Hold!
BUT
Why must I carry a mantel that was not meant for me to carry?
Especially not alone
Where is my Strong Black Man…… the one God crafted me from
I don't want to be HOH
That is not what I was made to be
Just let me a woman……as God created me
Strong in my own right
But not as a man
A supporter, nurturer, caregiver and all
Creating that environment of Love
Just let me be a woman
So Real Black Man
Stand up!!
Please take this mantel from me
I will not hold a grudge
Come into my life
Make me feel safe, secure, and protected
Please take your rightful place
Upon your Kingly throne
I will gladly place this crown upon your head
And take my place beside you….but never ahead
A Real Strong Black Woman will never take your place
She does not need to outshine her man
She will always show respect to her Strong black Man

That Kinda Love

I've found that school girl makes you blush and giggle
Kinda Love
Attached to that grown woman need of trust and consistency
Kinda Love
This man got me school girl skipping
Writing Me + Him = Forever
Kinda Love
Sending earthquake like shocks through my brain with his intelligence
While calming my spirit with just a simple touch
Kinda Love
We got that best friend, homey, ride or die, faith in God, you and I till the end
Kinda Love
That ooey gooey mushy but yet so serious super sexy
Kinda Love
Forged in mutual respect
Kinda Love
Keep it real and 100
Kinda Love
Got me asking what you want for dinner baby
Kinda Love
I've found that uplifting
I got ya back mama
Kinda Love
That got me blushing and giggling heart warm and protected
Kinda Love
Yeah……
I think I'm in Love

CHAPTER FOUR
TRANSFORMATION

ABSOLUTELY AMAZING
BEAUTIFULLY BEFITTING
TO BE
CREATIVELY CRAFTED
MY TRANSFORMATION

JUST ME

I am me- Uniquely made

He took me in His hands

For He is the potter and I am the clay

Shaped, carved, and molded me

Beginning the process of making me…… perfectly me

Placed in the fire

Harden by life

I am still me- Uniquely made

By His hands

Weathering from the storms may have left cracks and chips

But flaws and all

I am still A Masterpiece

Outwardly scarred with beauty eradiating from within

Far more precious than gold, rubies, diamonds or pearls

Uniquely designed with a purpose

I can only be me…

Put on this earth with a call

You may not understand my walk

But He understands it all

So do not judge my rough exterior

For I was made to endure and break down walls

So you see …

I stand tall

Flaws and All

Uniquely made and Called

Can't Stop

Eyes wide open

Time to walk in

My callin

Pain, burdens, and hardships

All of that I'm about to flip

She is a better woman

Here is where it will begin

Being an awesome mother

First priority

I am it

For my kids there is no other

Gotta lead with authority

For their lives will be my fame to glory

Only that can tell my true story

DEAR FUTURE

DEAR FUTURE,

I WILL BRING LIGHT INTO YOUR DARKNESS
ILLUMINATING EVERY PART OF YOUR BEING

YOU WILL BE MY MOON AND I YOUR SUN
EXPLORING NEW GALAXIES AND CREATING NEW WORLDS

YOU ALREADY KNOW WHAT IT IS
NOTHING MORE TO BE SAID

LOVE YOUR FUTURE,
SUNSHINE

You Make Me Happy

When I hear your voice or see your smile
You make me happy
When you triumph over life's obstacles
You make me happy
When you crack a joke with your silly self
You make me happy
When you tell me about your day
You make me happy
When you call me just to check on me
You make me happy
When you're sitting there gazing at the TV or video game
You make me happy
When you write that new song or story
You make me happy
Seeing you grow and become an awesome person
You make me happy
Watching you succeed at life
You make me happy
Just being you, you, and you
Makes me happy
My children, Steffen, Myliscia, and James
Make me happy!

I Love ME

Absolutely Amazing
Beautifully Befitting
to be
Creatively Crafted
Divinely Destined
toward
Extraordinarily Exceptional
Favor & Fervently
Gracious Glory
Honestly Humble
Insatiably Iconic
Justifiably Jazzy
Kinky Knotted hair
Lusciously Lovely
&
Marvelously Mastered
Naturalistic Nubian
whose
Openly Opinionated
Poetically
Precious
&
Queendom Qualified
Righteously Righteous
Sublimely Sexy
with a
Taste of Tantalizingly
Undeniable Uniqueness
Voluptuously Vibrant
Whimsically Wonderful
Xuberantly Xenodochy
Youthfully Yappy
and
Zestfully Zealous

I LOVE ME SOME ME!

My Love Song

I still love you....
Kick me when I'm down...I still love you
Leave me when I need you most...I still love you
Attempt to tarnish my character...I still love you
Talk about me behind my back...I still love you
Abuse me with your words and actions...I still love you
Molest me of my innocence...I still love you
No matter what is thrown at me you cannot destroy my loving
heart or steal my joy
My heart was created to love and nourish others
And through it all my heart keeps on beating strong
Because God still loves me
Through all of my mistakes, failures, and falls
He still loves me....
So
I still love you

Aliscia Melton

She is....

From her very essence illuminates an effervescent bright light
She is the definition of woman
Created to stand out and lead
She is the giver of life
Teacher
Nurturer
Beauty, Brains, and Charisma abundantly pour from her being
Her very presence alone would knock the "ag' out of swag
She is a creature of elegance
A supreme being bringing righteousness and brilliance with just the stroke of her hand
One glimpse of her sun rays lights up the whole room
You have no other choice but to respect her essence
For she is so bright one must wear shades when in her presence
No need to fry your eye retinas
Her footsteps leave a trail of sweet sunny warmth with every step that she takes
Leaving a trail of sunflowers in her remembrance
Once experienced you could never erase the memory of her extraordinary image
Powerful and humble is she in her stance of virtue
She is me.....
She is you....
The Beautiful Black Woman

She Rises

She started off as a simple seed
As small as a mustard seed
Planted in the dark, cold, and sometimes dry barren soil of life
There she grew
Withstanding
Enduring
Accepting
Embracing
The ever changes of the seasons
Receiving the love of sun, while enduring the heat of its often burning razes
Drowning in the precipitation of the earth, known as rain, allowing it to quench her dry roots
Dancing and swaying to the high velocity of the wind as it dries, refreshes, and cleanses her growing limbs covered in beautiful foliage
She stands well-grounded in mother earth
Taking her position of authority
Encompassing all that is considered "bad weather" to strengthen and build her
Look at her now
This beautiful creation of life, laid out in the wilderness
A strong woman
Using what was thrown at her for destruction to
Grow
Flourish
&
Surmount Above All
To be a witness and covering to all women following in her foot steps

Old Me, New Me

<u>Old Me</u>

Cynical
Walls up
Perceived Strength
Nothing can touch or harm me
Confident
Serious
No nonsense approach to life
Covered in the dark hues of Red, Black, and grey

<u>New Me</u>

Positive
Strong
Carefree
Silly
Affectionate
Free-Spirited (kinda) lol
Playful
Passionate
Loving
Imaginative
Artistic
Covered in the vibrant hues of Pink, Yellow, blue, and Orange

My cloudy days have just produced its end product…….Me
A beautiful vibrant Rainbow

SUNSHINE BLACKROSE

Sunshine BlackRose
A Woman of Distinction
Hailing from the Distinguished Royal Family
A soldier illuminating an effervescent bright light
Always on the battlefield geared up and ready to fight
I use my pen to purge my mind spillage
Giving precious poetic life to feed my village
See I'm Queendom Qualified
&
Divinely Destined
To
Educate and lead the masses
This is why I stand tall and defend the masses
The anointing placed on me is like that outta this world galactical Fiyah!
That some look up to and admire
You see, I started from the gutta ....Now I'm here
Stimulating ya mind with my ink
Giving you no choice but to think
Taking you to the school of Sunshine BlackRose
Betta than any 4 year college, this fact no one can oppose
You see, I started from the gutta...Now I'm here
Where I rise
With my head held high
Carrying the burdens of others on my shoulders
Uplifting and educating nations all before sunrise
Clothed in Strength and Honor
With my mouth full of wisdom and kindness
And my pen fully equipped with bullets of Knowledge
Because I bow to the King of all Kings
He has blessed me with this verbal gift that stings...
Opening up the eyes, mind, and heart
Letting people know they can be set apart
You see this is not just a gift
But an art
Giving inspiration so people can see they can have a fresh start
If they just lift their hands
Open up their hearts
And confess that they understand
Jesus Christ died on the cross
To give them everlasting life
To be a cover and comfort in their time of strife
I am Sunshine BlackRose
A vessel of the Lord
Strong
Confident
One that could never be ignored

POETIC TONGUES

Speaking in Poetic Tongues
As the voice in my head
Gives utterance to my pen
My mind spillage overflowing yet again
My ink a crimson red
Just like the blood that was shed
Freeing us all from sin
So a new life can begin
My ink is that thread
For me
To become free
Cleansing my mind
So I can truly see
And not be blind
Completely Unconfined
Speaking in Poetic Tongues
As new breath is flowing in my lungs
Cleansing me from within
Drawing me in
Closer to The One
The only begotten Son
Speaking in Poetic Tongues
Has got me sprung
And my pen bringing to life
Verses that are unsung
Musical notes unstrung
A rhythmic language
Understood by a chosen few
Who
Knew…

That Speaking in Poetic Tongues
Could wash you white as snow
Giving you that flow
That could set your whole world aglow
Allowing you to reach a new plateau
With a fresh streamline flow
That is so above the status quo
Speaking in Poetic Tongues
As the voice in my head
Gives utterance to my pen
Raising me from the dead
As only it can
Now I will end
As I began
Bowing my head
Speaking in Poetic Tongues
Saying....
Amen

ITS TIME FOR WAR

Wake up in the morning, Time to pray
Must strap on my armor, No time to delay
We all know the passage; do this in remembrance
But as a soldier, It's about more than just attendance
Principalities, powers, and rulers of the darkness,
spiritual wickedness, have me thinking I'm not ready for battle
But by the blood, it's time to make the devil's voice fearfully rattle
Fear the child of God who's prepared for war and ready to battle
Who's wit me!
Who's Ready!
It's time for war!
Grab those boots, shod those feet, let's let the devil know we ain't accepting defeat
Shine up that breast plate
I want all to see the righteousness of the Holy Spirit all over me!!
1 Peter 5:8 tells me
The devil is like a roaring lion seeking me out trying to devour.
I'm girding myself with truth
Be sober
Be vigilant
Who's wit me!
Who's ready!
It's time for war!
The devil had me stuck playing defense
Putting on my salvational helmet and blocking with this shield of faith
But its 4th down and GodSquad is on offense
Hebrew 4:12
The word of God is quick, powerful, and sharper than a 2 edge sword.
Watch out Lucifer, I'm ready for war!
Who's wit me!
Who's ready!
It's time for war!
So all my soldiers get your armor on
Get in formation
Cuz Godsquad is marching out
We're on the front line
Geared up for war
Who's wit me!
Who's ready!
Cuz it's time for War!

Epilogue

Planted Seed Part 2

My child hearken your heart unto my words

Receive the gift of life thru the shedding of my blood and Words

You were blessed and touched by my hand before you were formed in your mother's womb

Because you were marked with my blood covered crest,

You were targeted early on in his attempts of destruction

Robbing, stealing, and creating roadblocks

Planting seeds of inferiority, abandonment, and mistrust

BUT…. All things work together for good to them that love me, and are called….

And as I stated in my Word, weapons may form but they shall not prosper

So while the deceiver thought he was trying to kill you,

He could not understand nor see the greater picture

That I allowed him access to you, one of my soldiers early on in your training

His plan of fear, strife, and ultimate death was just an obstacle course in my boot camp

Training and equipping you to be used for My glory!

With every lie and deception and seed of brokenness planted

I in return watered and nurtured the seeds with love and truth

Transforming them into seeds of

Courage, Endurance, Patience, Understanding, Love, temperance, Peace, and Fortitude

That strengthened your soul and spirit man even before you understood your purpose

And that you were a tri-dimensional woman

I saw your struggle and hurt

It was I speaking to your heart that created that thirst within you

To find your purpose and the answer to the greater meaning of life

I saw your desire to find me, placing just the right ones on your path to guide you to me

I was overjoyed as I watched you give your life back to be me, be reborn thru me

Acknowledging me as your Rock and Salvation

Now you understand why every attempt of destruction and suicide was blocked

For I know the thoughts I have toward you, thoughts of peace and not of evil.

To give you an expected end……. Working within my ranks glorifying me.

I have created your bio

And it is now time for you to walk upright in it:

Soldier in The Army of the Lord,

Charged to create, equip, and uplift God's people with the knowledge and application of what it means to be an effective soldier on the battle field.

Representing and warring in the natural and spiritual for the Commander in Chief,

Jesus Christ.

You are a

Prayer Warrior

Poet

Author

Business owner

Outreach Activist

Clothing Designer

Mentor

All for the Glory of the Most High

King of all Kings

He might win some but he just lost one

Acknowledgments

I would like to start off acknowledging and thanking my business partner Ericka Taylor for all of her help during this process. A huge thanks and gratitude goes to Christian and Archon Editing and Review for their great work, timeliness, and expertise. BRPP Originals/Custom Designs and Kim Morrow, I thank you and so appreciate you for blessing me with this recreation of my book cover and all the other things you have done for me.

I thank all of my family and friends that supported me during this process and gave their advice, listening ears, and took the time to read my work. I love you all very dearly. Andrea Julian you know without you only God knows where I would be. Thanks to Chester Roberson for encouraging me and pushing me to step out of my comfort zone and always challenging me to perfect my craft.

A big shout out to my sisters, Niesy, Shari, and Toya and my big brother Charles "Woody", love you guys to life! Of course, thank you and love to my parents, Louis Melton and Sharon Melton for bringing me into this world.

I would like to extend my appreciation to the Mann that was the first to inspire and encourage my writing and who my first "mind spillage" was about. Things may not have turned out how we imagined but I thank you and God for the lessoned learned from it all.

Lastly, but far from least, my children; Steffen, Myliscia, and James you guys are my reason for living and inspiration every day. Thank you guys for loving mommy just the way I am as I love and accept you all just the way you are.

About the Author

Aliscia began writing as a youth by journaling and creating stories. It was a way for her to deal with her emotions and turbulent upbringing. She later picked writing back up when she became involved with the Youth Ministry at church. She would write short plays, speeches, and poems for the children to recite.

In 2012, Aliscia was re-introduced to poetry through friends and some personal struggles in her life. During this time she found solace in writing and her horizon was broadened
as she saw her life story being written out in poetic form, which she refers to as her "mind spillage". This caused her to share her work with others online and to eventually create a group through Facebook where all could come and freely express themselves in poetic form (Poetic Freedom Café).https://www.facebook.com/groups/Poeticfreedomcafe/

Aliscia has been featured on "The Literary Corner" a blog radio show where she shared her art of poetry and on Eloquently Speaking an online magazine http://eloquentlyspeaking.homestead.com/aliscia.html

She has also been featured as Poet of the month in Eloquently Speaking, a poetry group on Facebook and featured online at http://www.blacktopia.org/2015/05/books-sunshine-blackrose-from.html

Aliscia has been featured on The Top 15 of the Month on the website www.ellemclin.com , A Shared Format 4 Poets, over 8 times for several of her poetry pieces, sometime making the list multiple times in one month for different pieces.

Aliscia Melton is not only a poet but an entrepreneur, mentor, and community activist. For more information about Aliscia Melton, the renaissance woman, check out her personal website:www.alisciamelton.com